The Heather Doram
Caribbean Collection Coloring Book

ABOUT THE ARTIST

Heather Doram is a visual and performing artist from the beautiful country of Antigua and Barbuda. Her entire childhood was spent in the countryside; where she always found joy and endless inspiration in observing the flora, fauna, ocean, village life, and people around her. She also creates art that showcases her heritage and culture.

Her fanciful hand drawn illustrations will surely bring joy, peace, colour and creativity to your life. This collection invites you to explore her island home and discover it's beauty along the way.

Find Heather on Facebook and IG @heatherdoramart

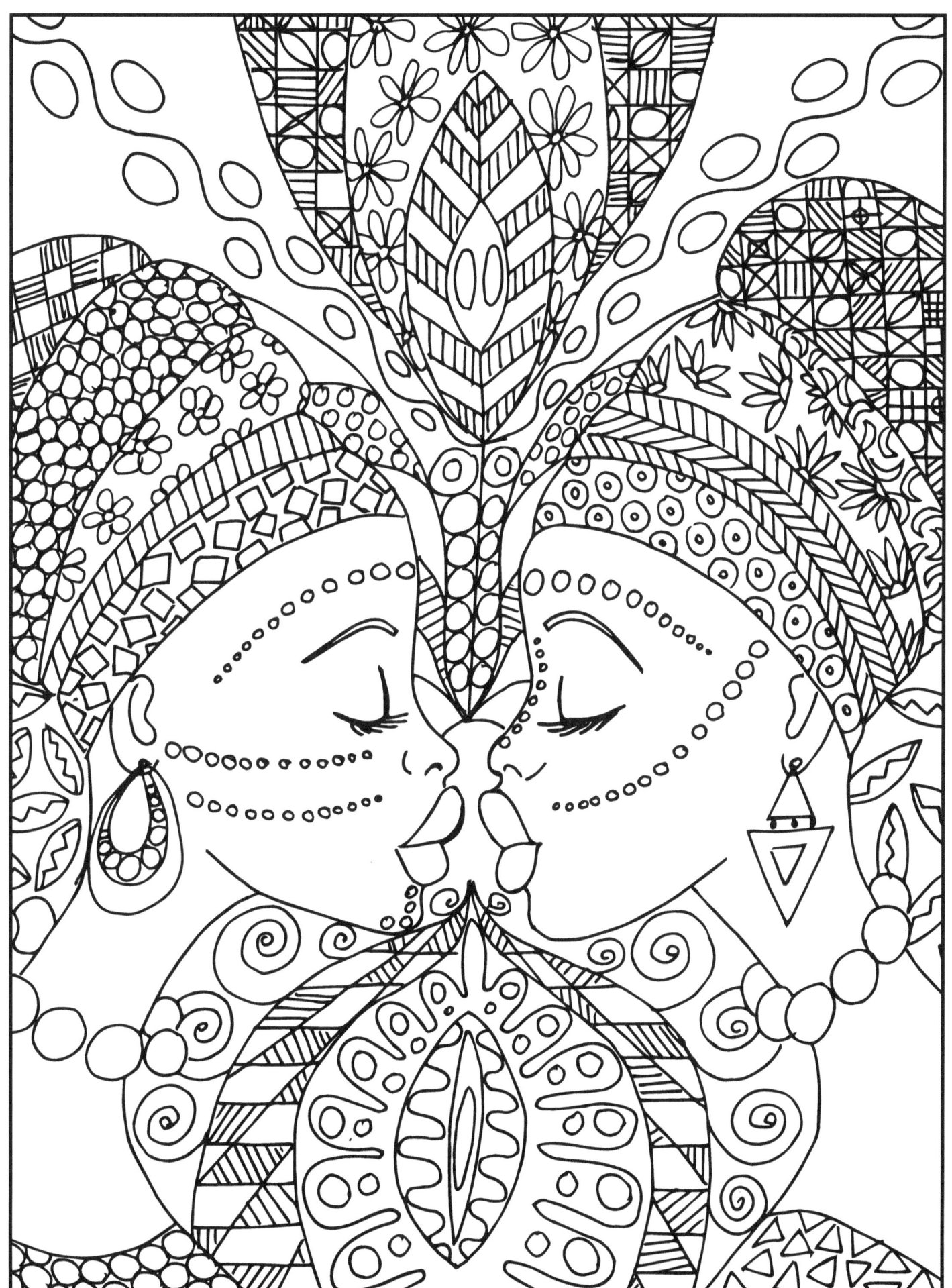

Caribbean Collection - HOMELAND

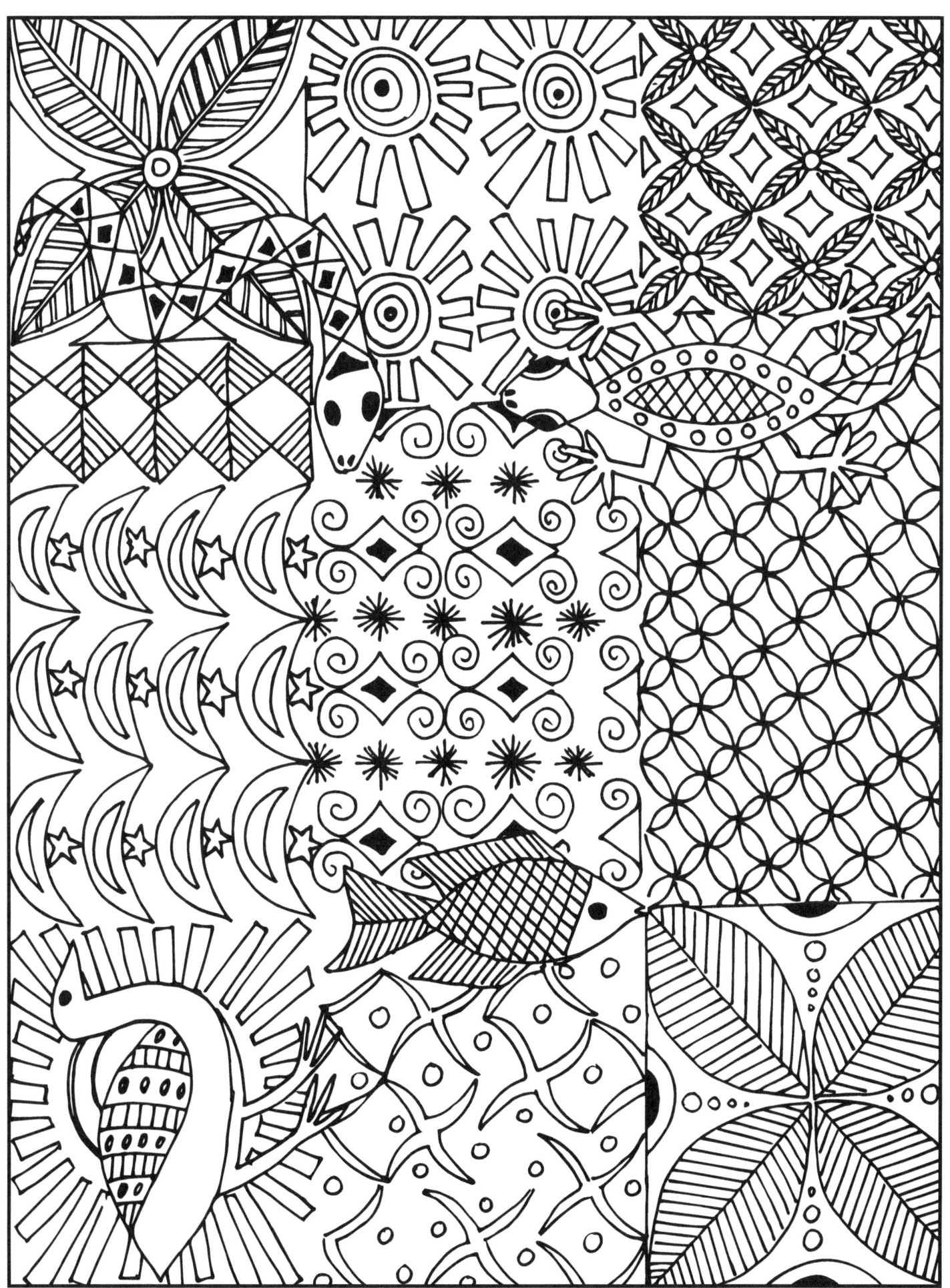

Caribbean Collection - HOMELAND

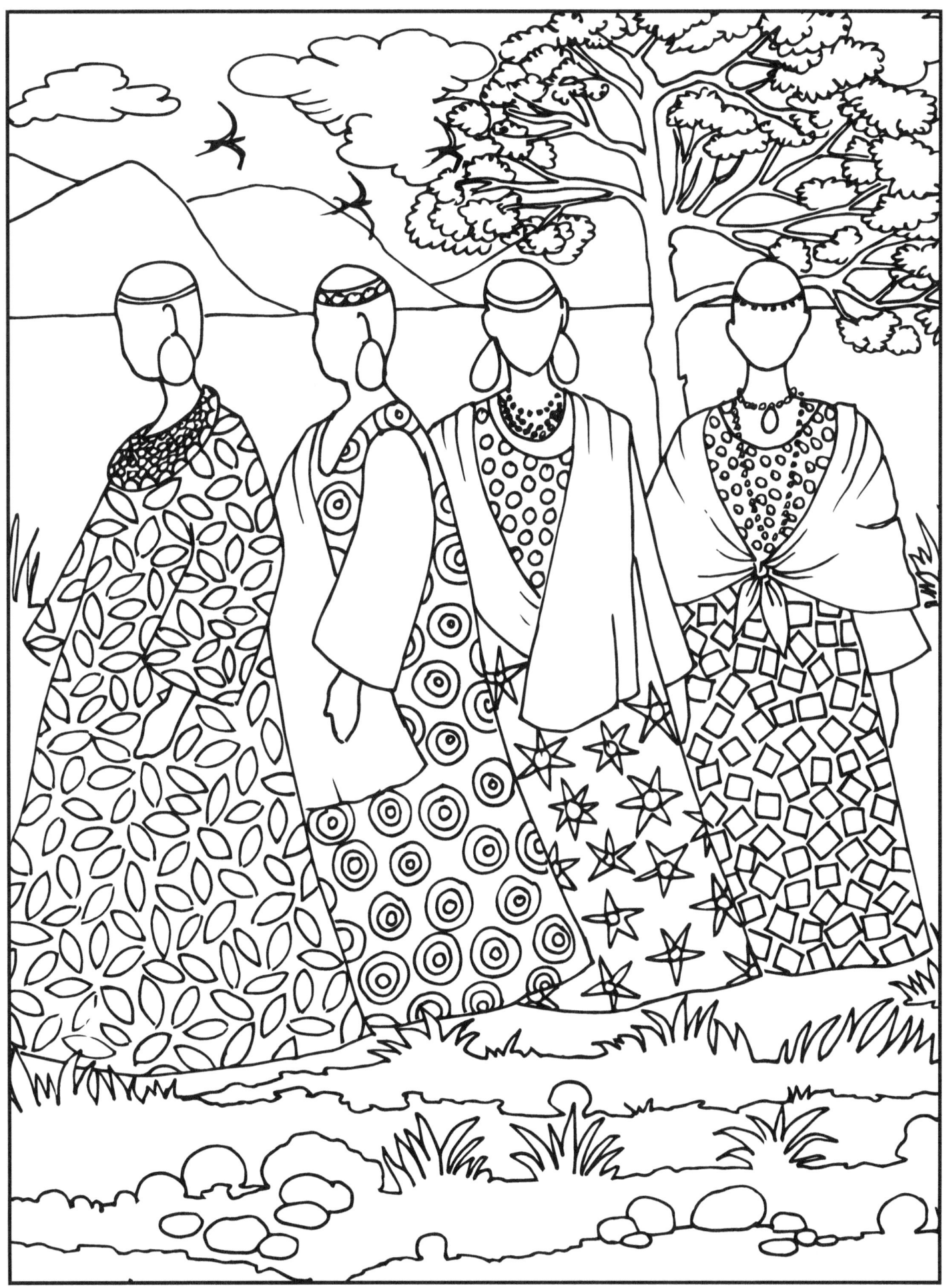

Caribbean Collection - HOMELAND

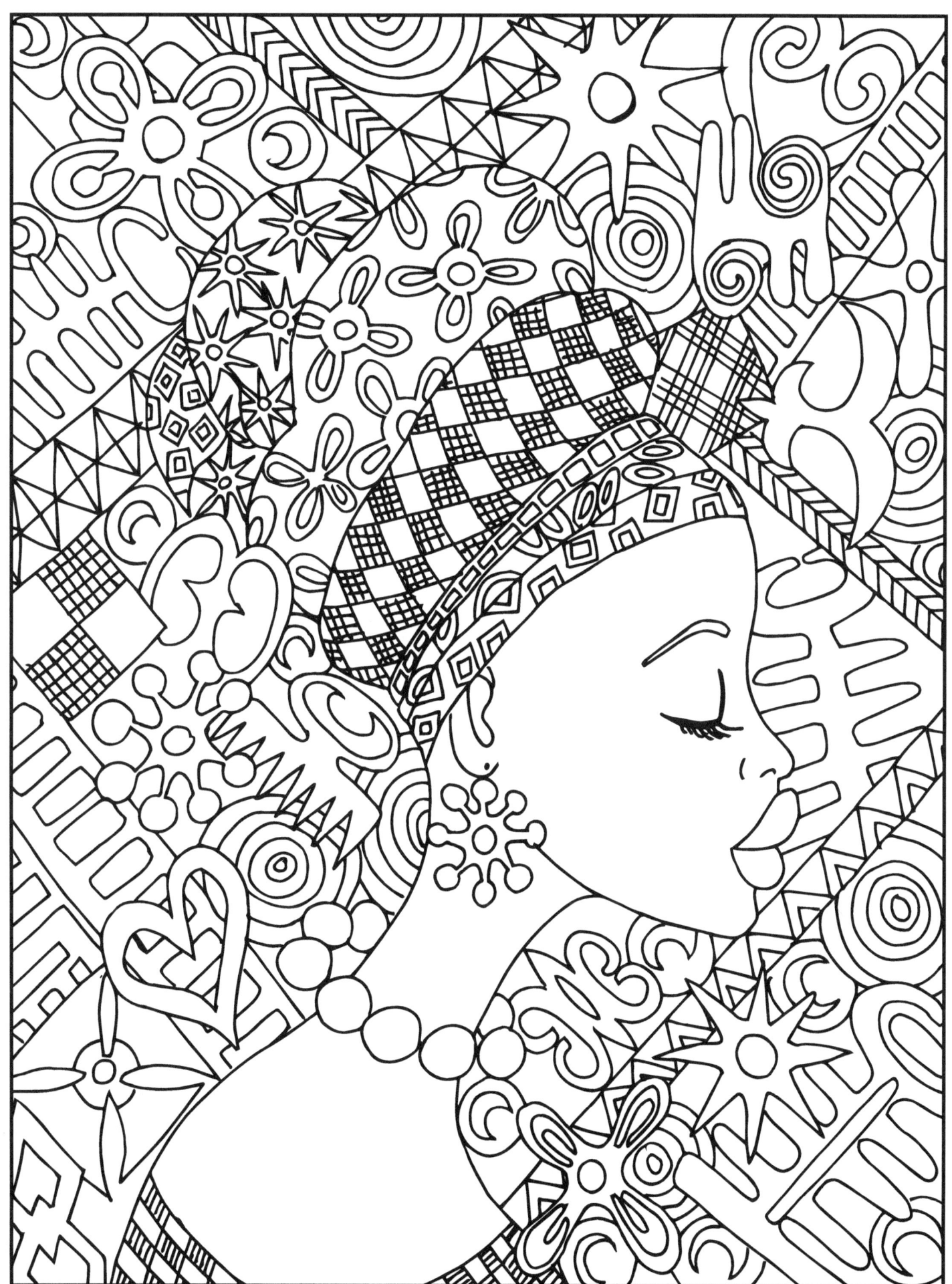

Caribbean Collection - HOMELAND

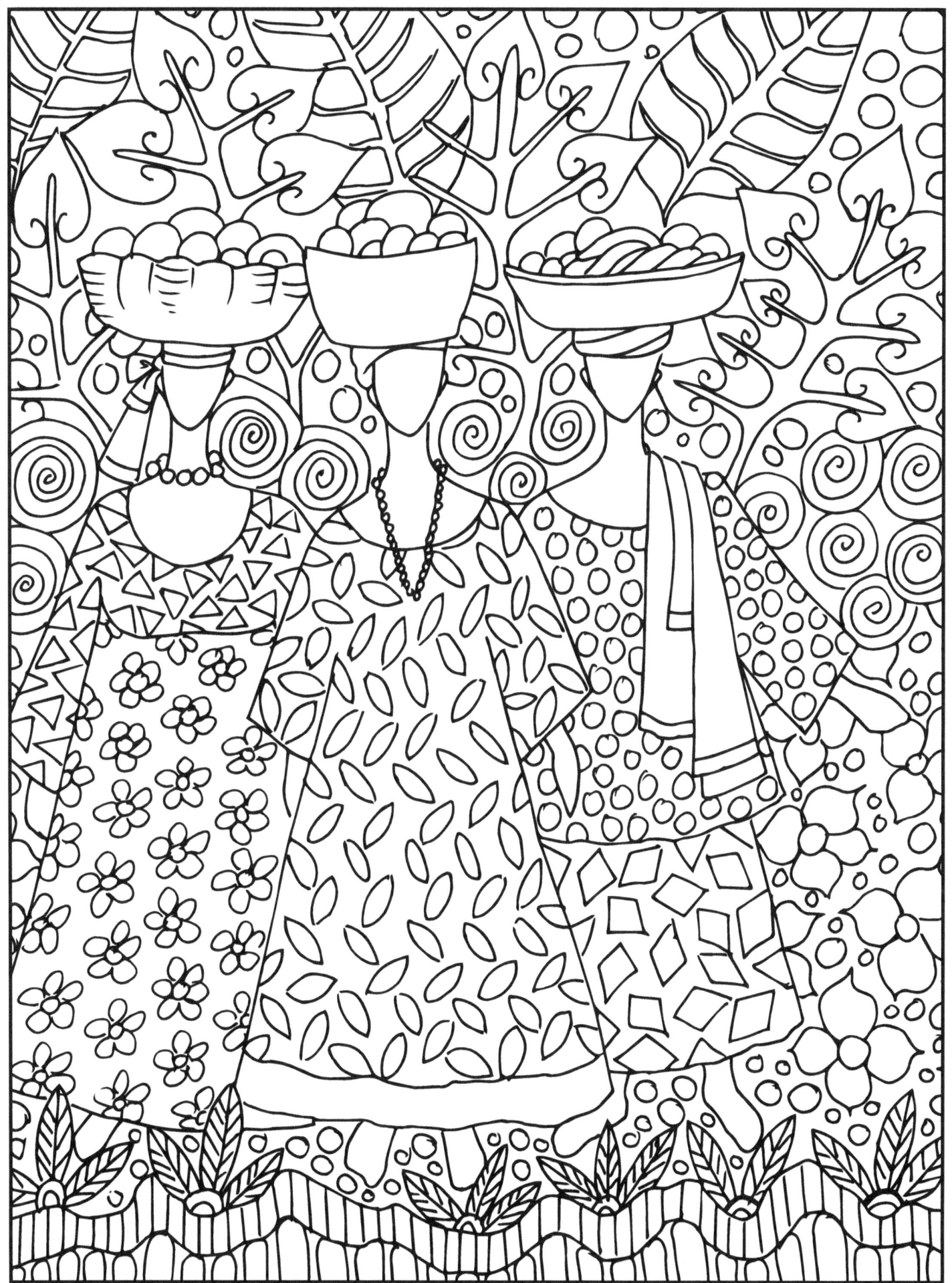

Caribbean Collection - HOMELAND

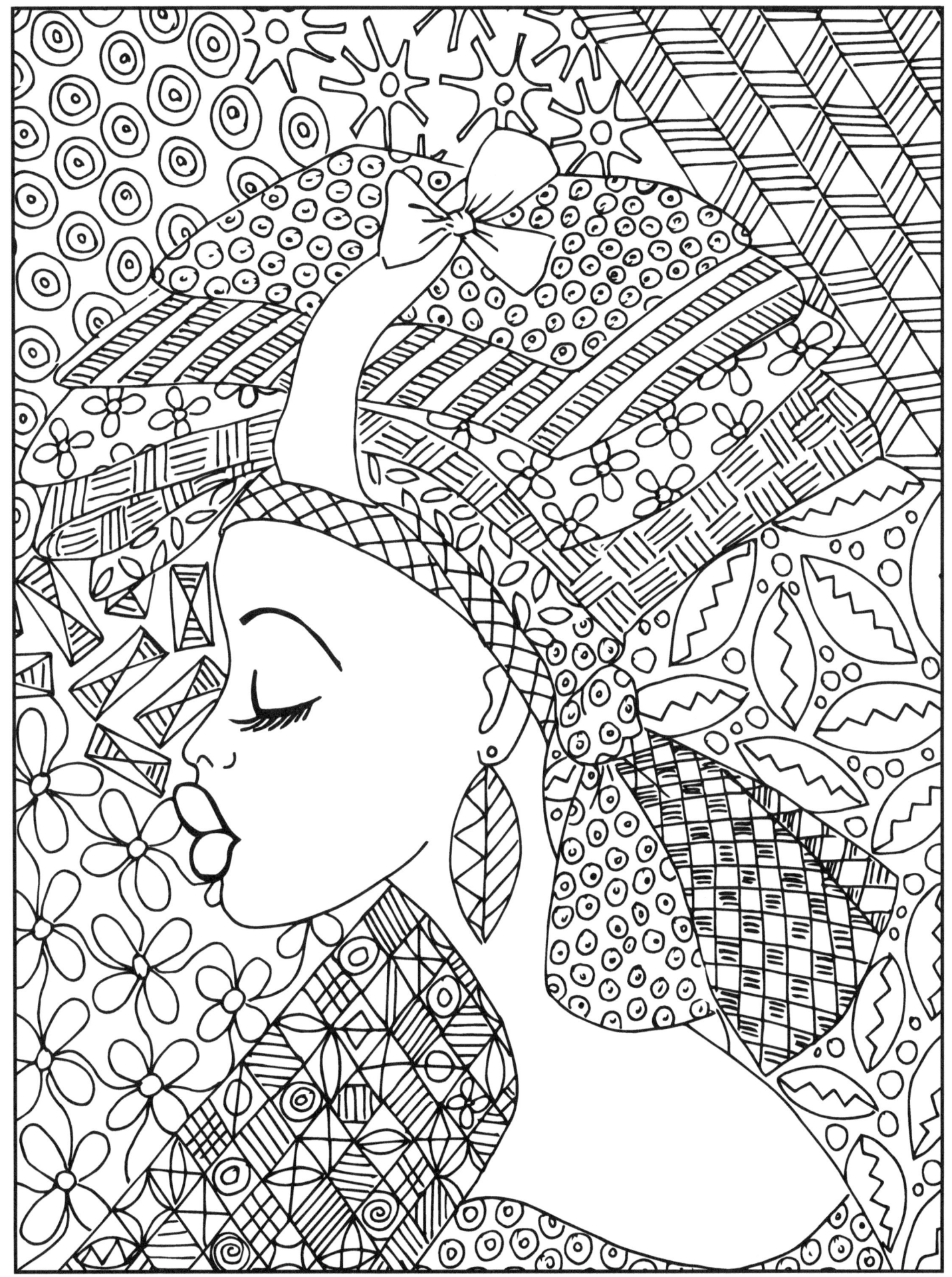

Caribbean Collection - HOMELAND

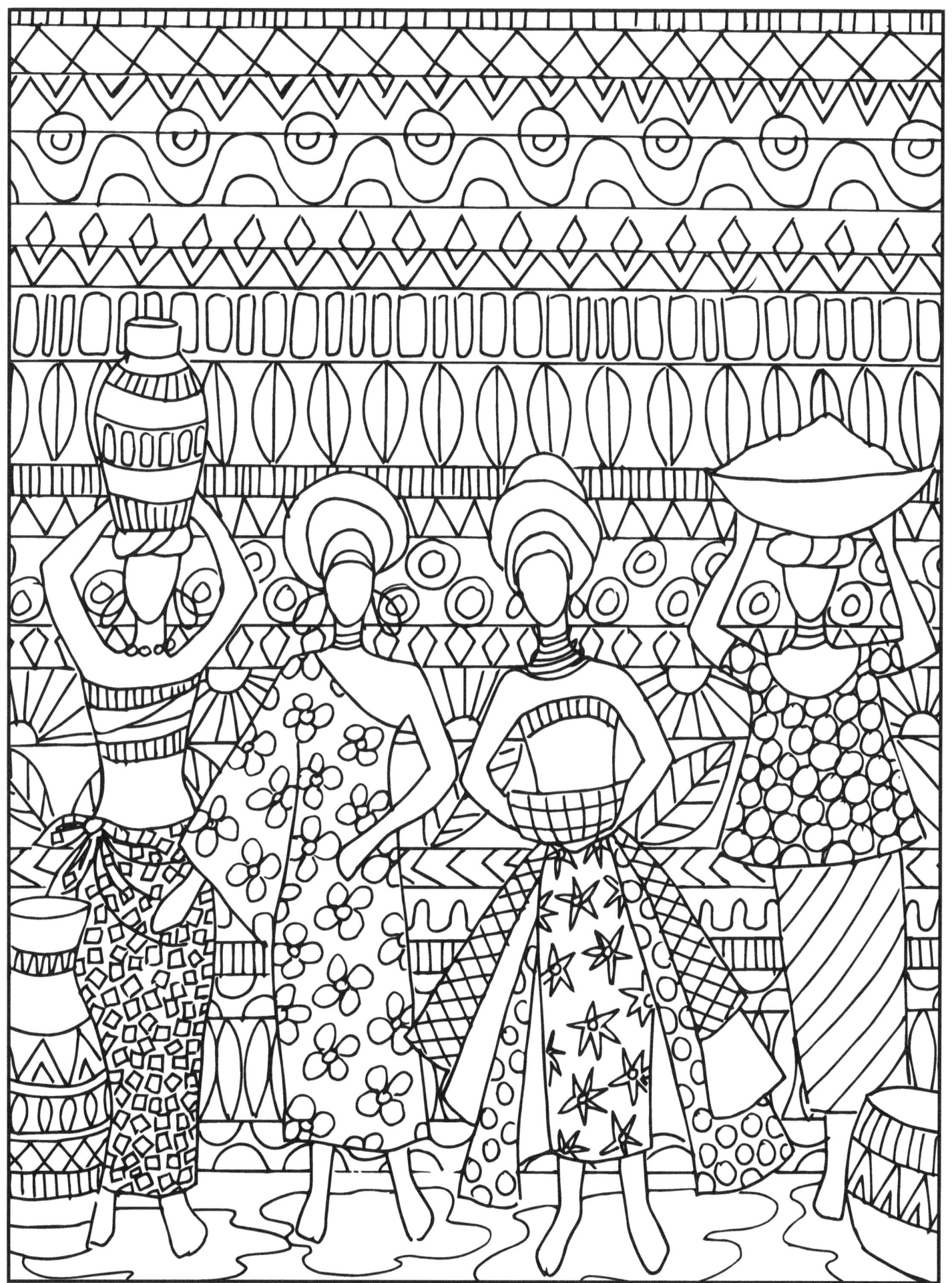

Caribbean Collection - HOMELAND

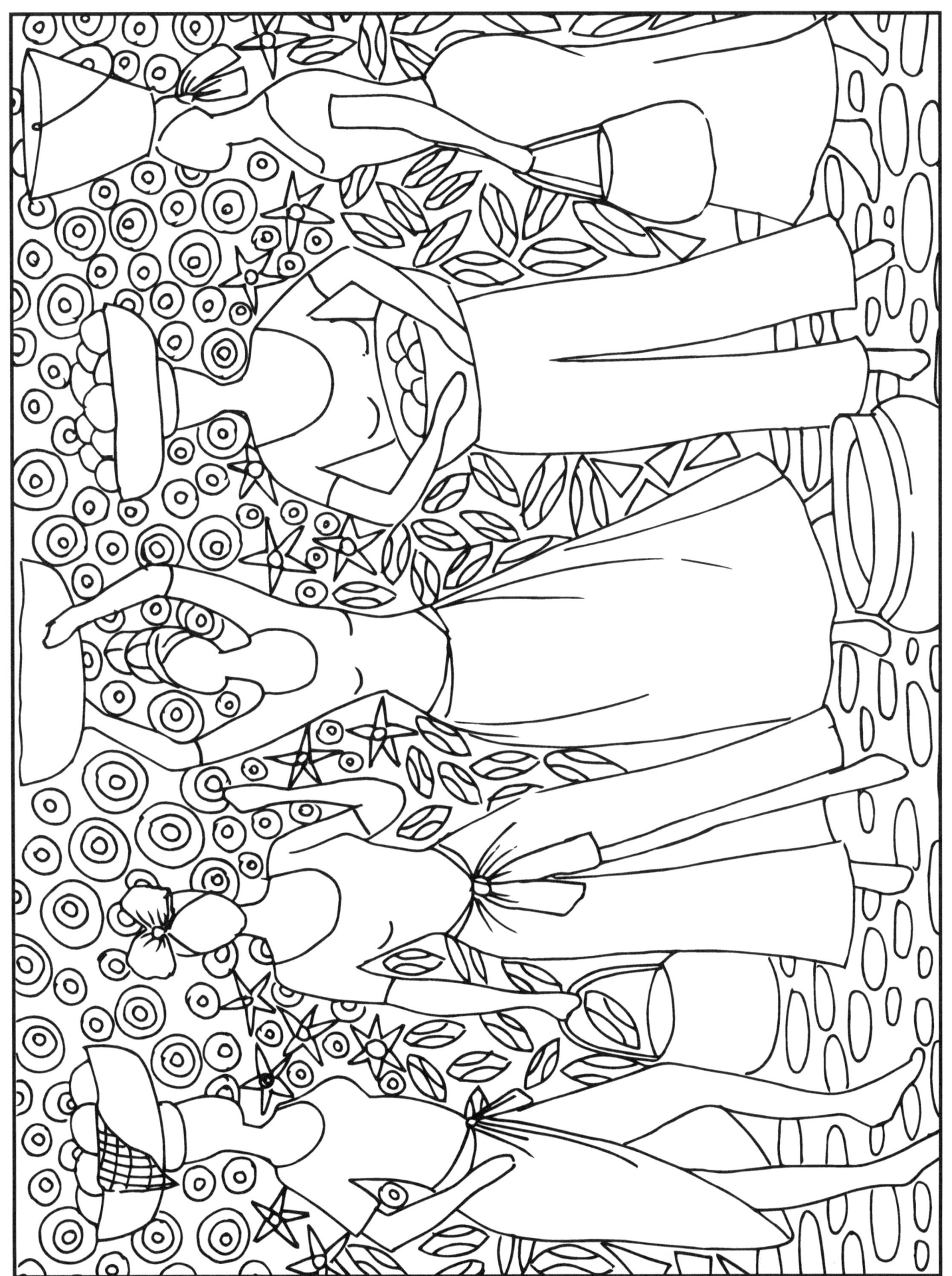

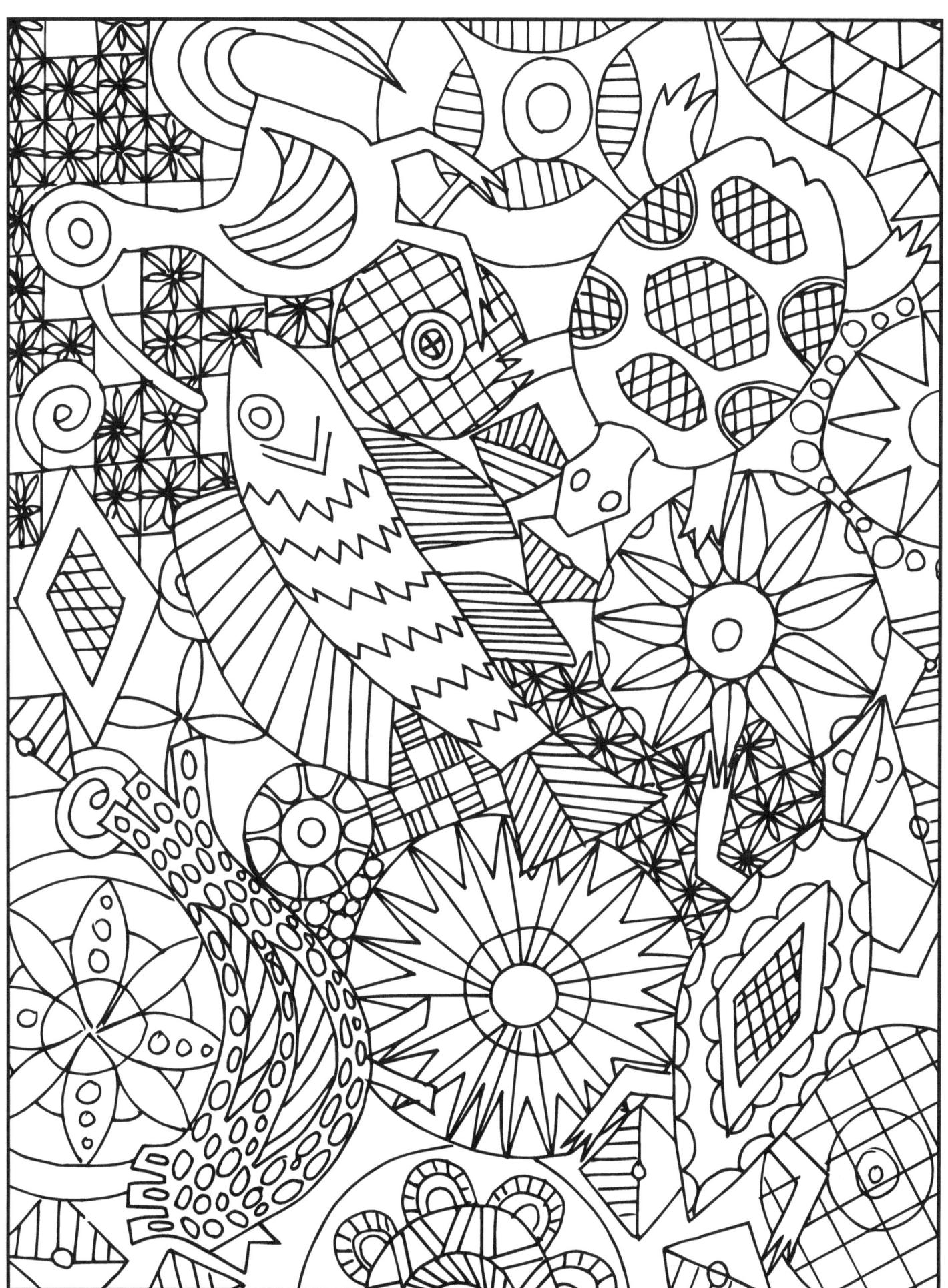

Caribbean Collection - HOMELAND

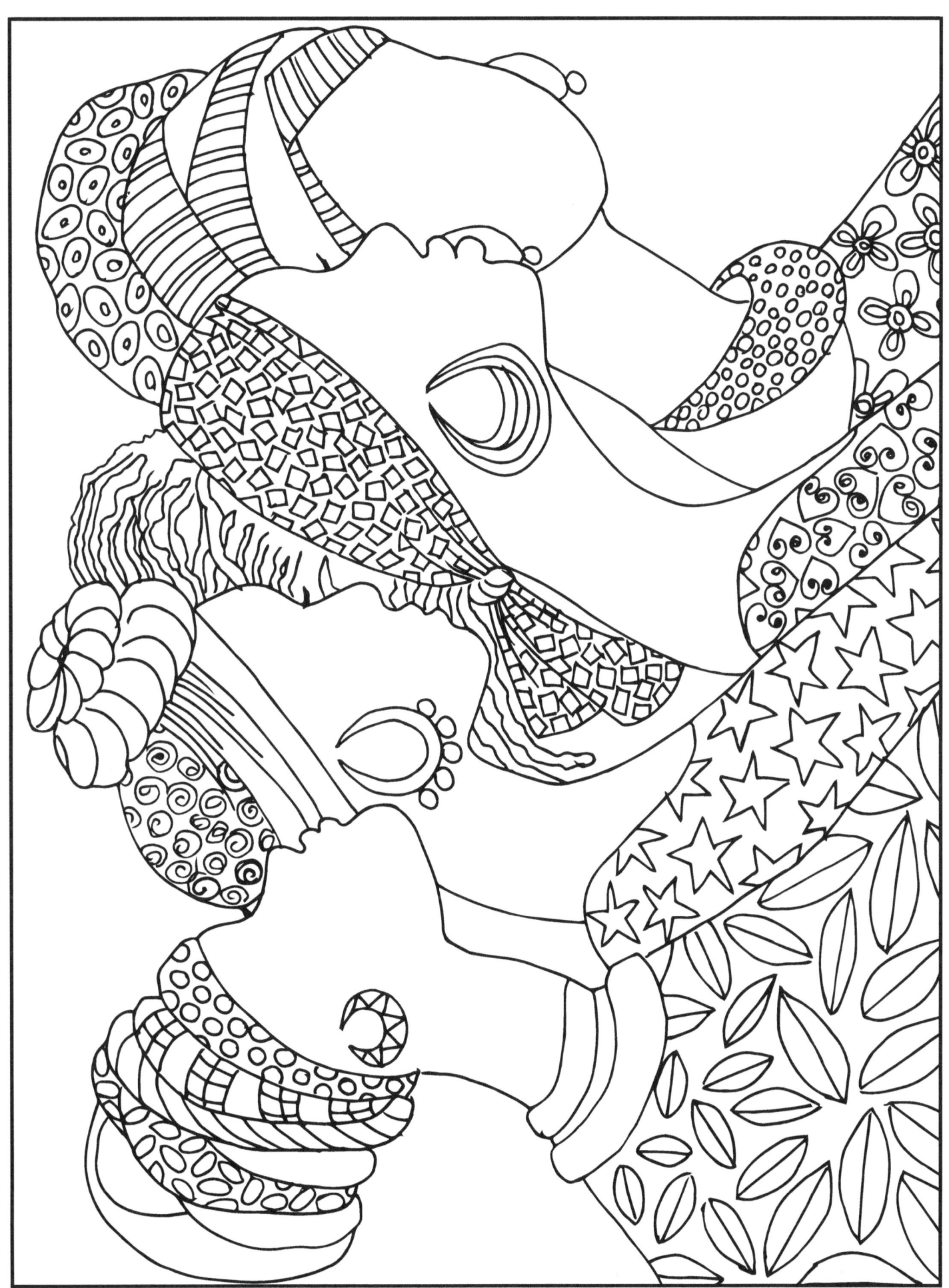

Caribbean Collection - HOMELAND

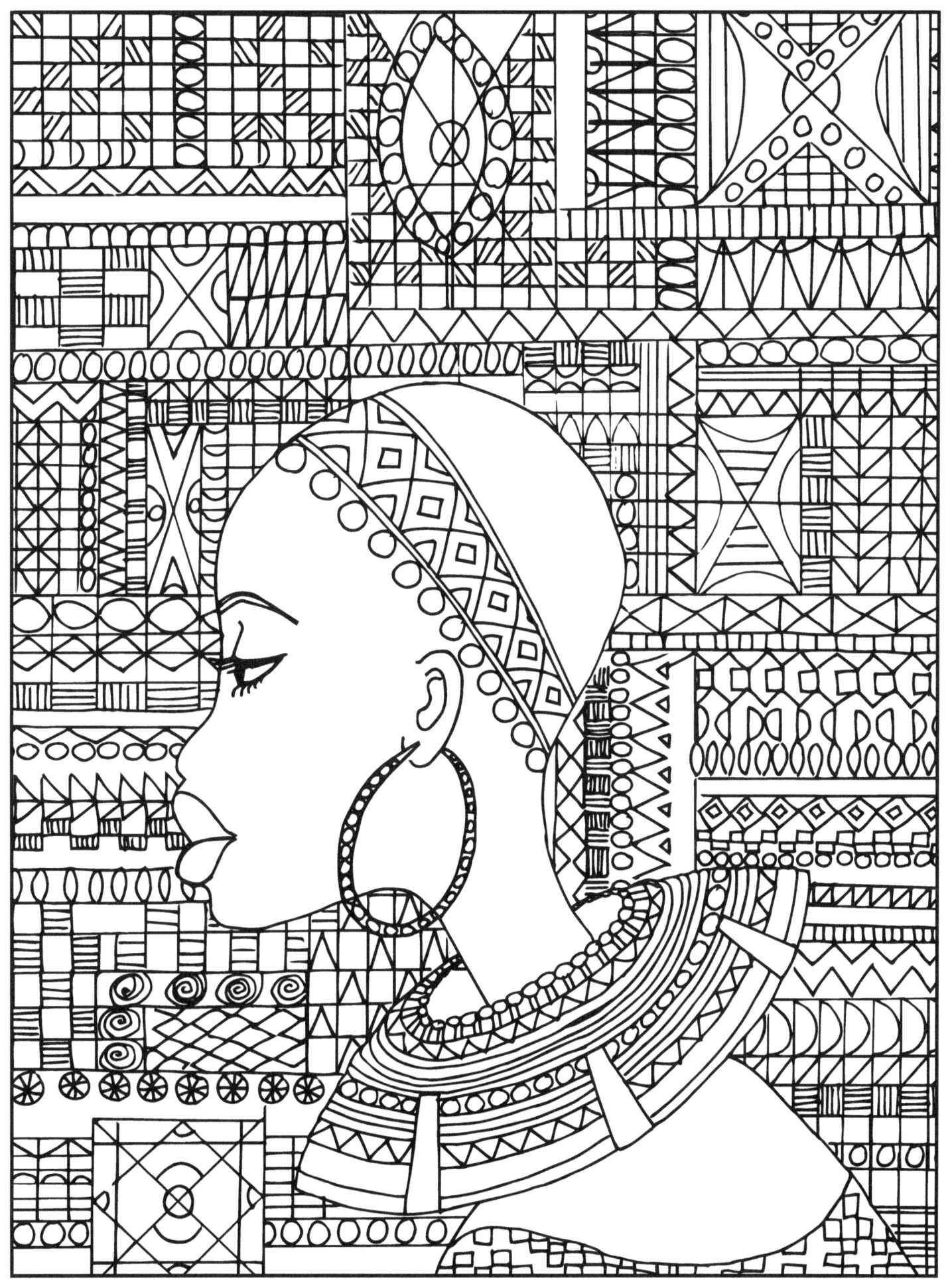

Caribbean Collection - HOMELAND

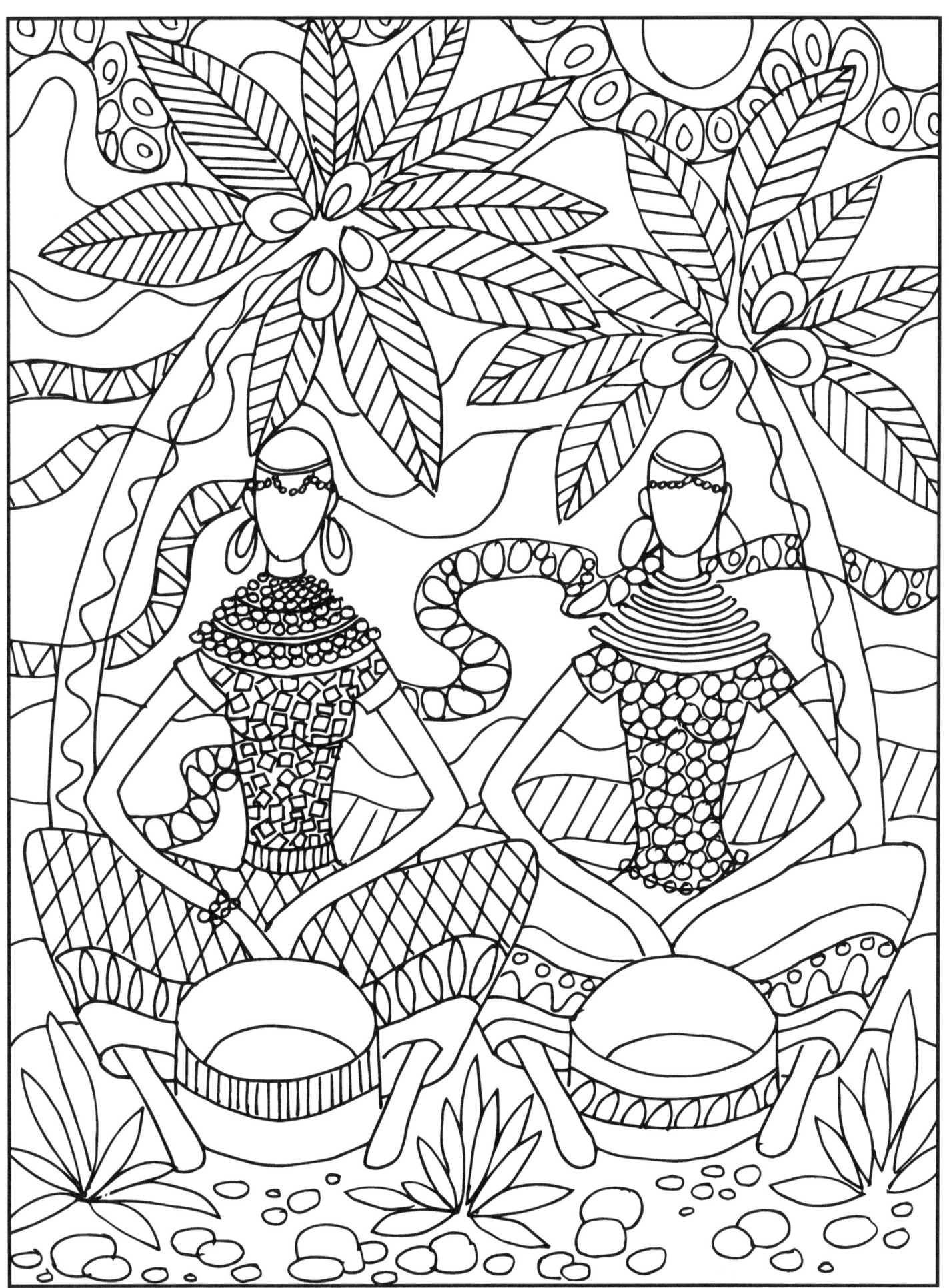

Caribbean Collection - HOMELAND

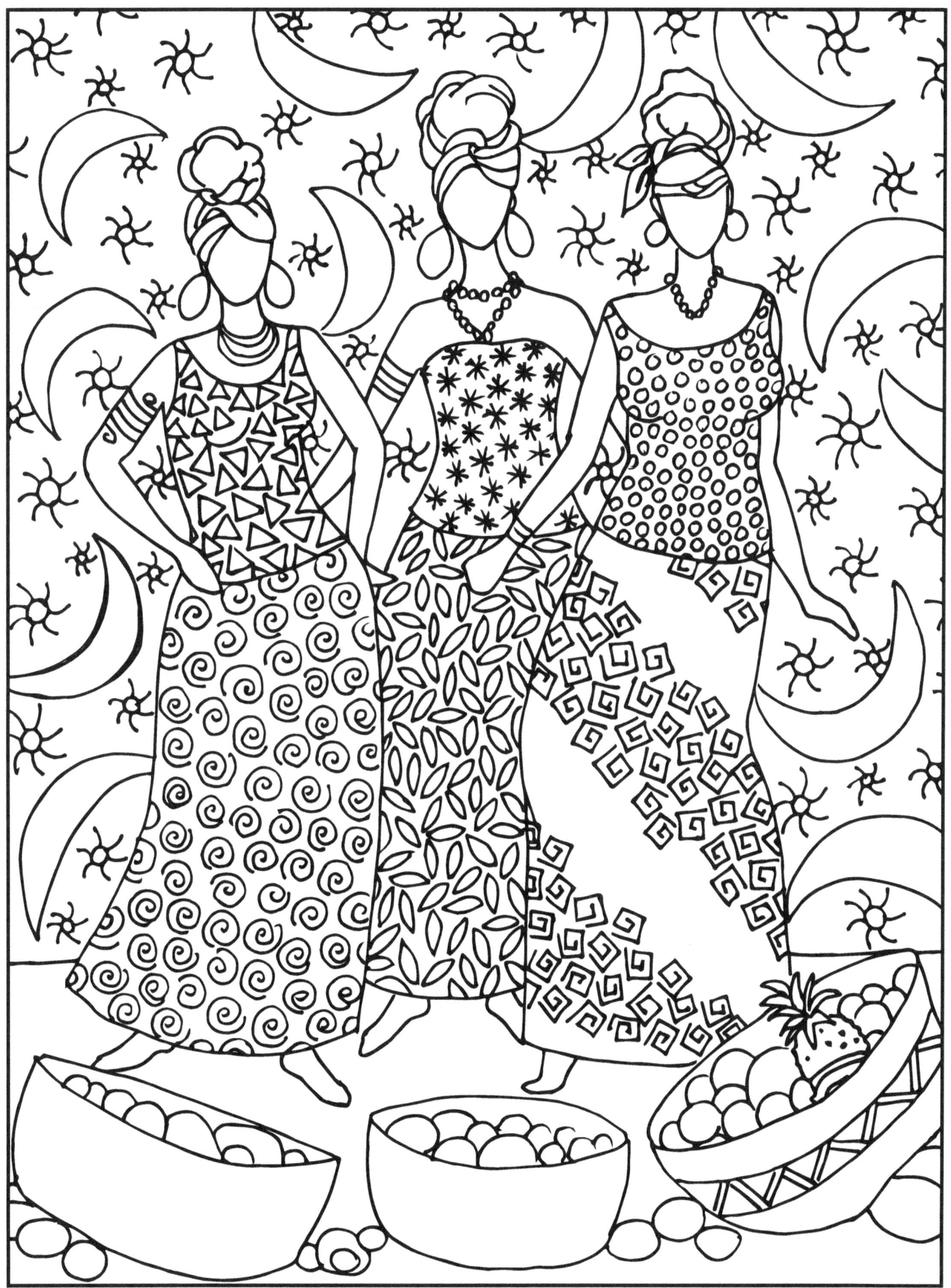

Caribbean Collection - HOMELAND

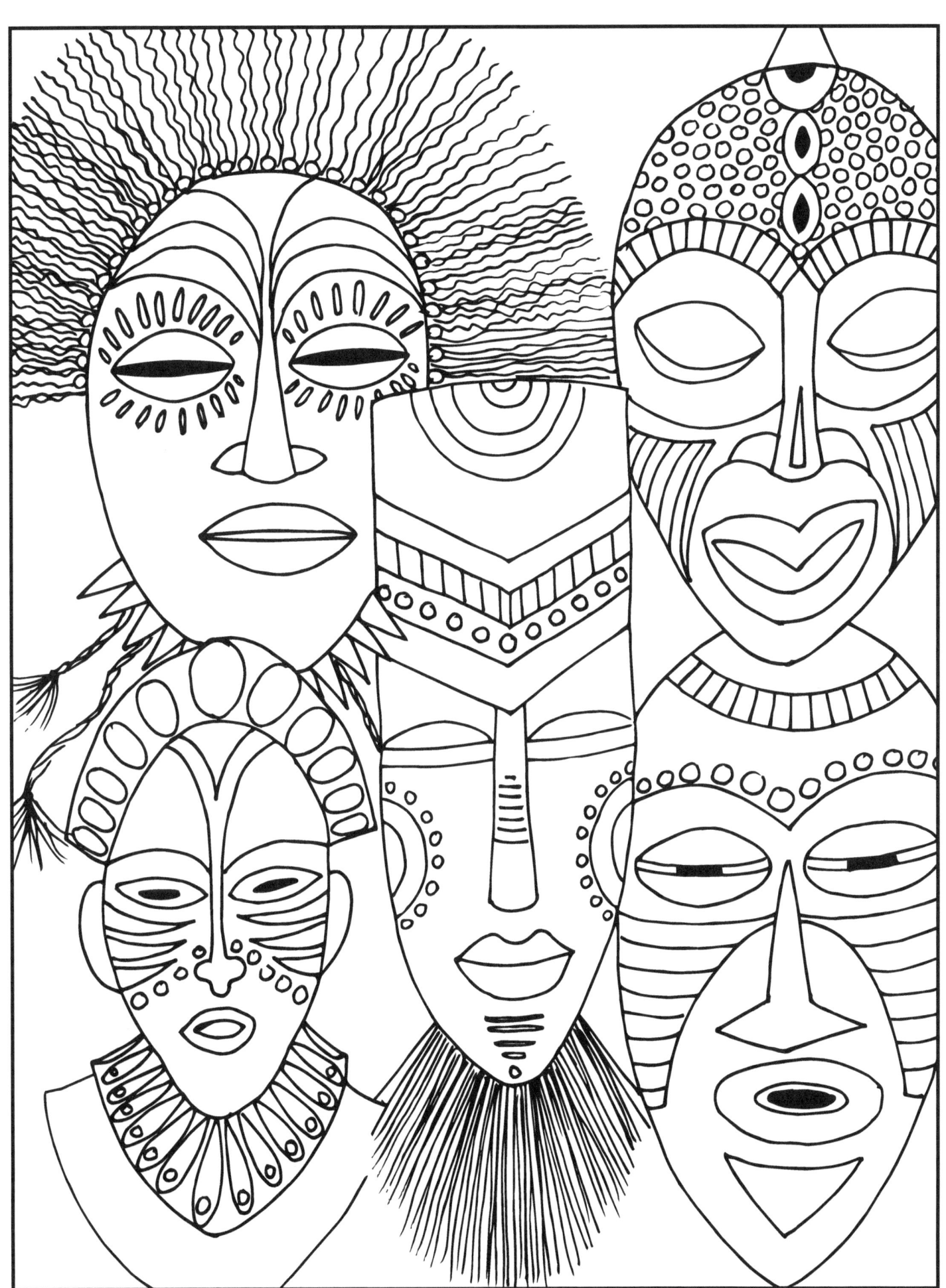

Caribbean Collection - HOMELAND

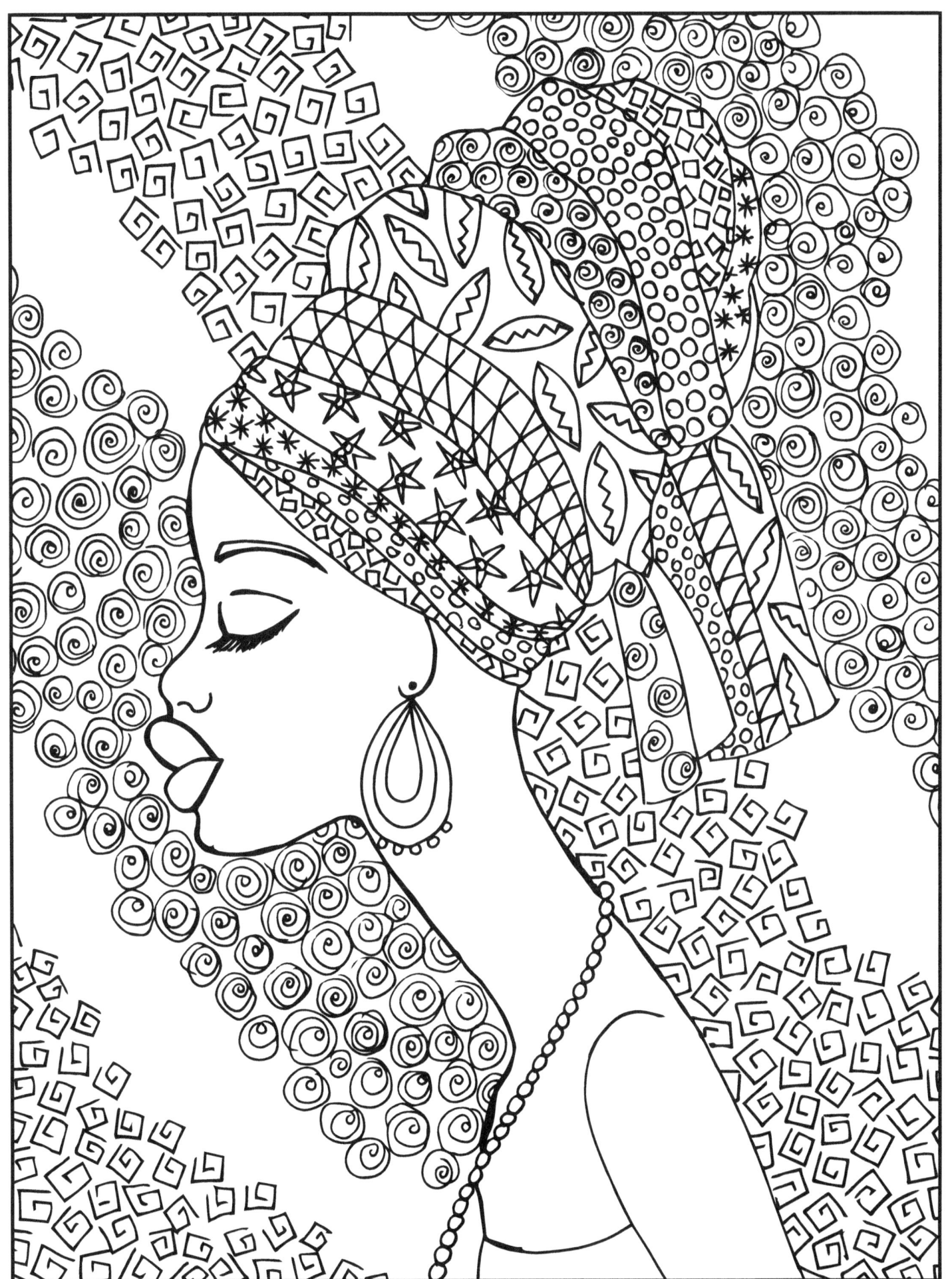